CW00707014

THE UNOFFICIAL

Johnny Depp

BY
Esme Hawes

This edition first published by
Parragon Book Service Ltd in 1996

Parragon Book Service Ltd
Unit 13–17 Avonbridge Trading Estate
Atlantic Road, Avonmouth
Bristol BS11 9QD

Produced by Magpie Books,
an imprint of Robinson Publishing

ISBN 0 75251 790 2

A copy of the British Library Cataloguing in Publication
Data is available from the British Library.

Typeset by Whitelaw & Palmer Ltd, Glasgow

EARLY YEARS

John Christopher Depp was born in Owensboro, Kentucky on 9 June 1963, the youngest of four children. They were a close family despite the fact that his brother, Dan, and one of his sisters, Christi, were the offspring of his mother's first marriage. They were a regular, small-town American family, living in a regular, small suburban house and sharing regular American aspirations. John Depp Sr was a city engineer who

Johnny Depp

worked for the local council while his mother, Betty Sue, was employed as a waitress in a local café. Her 'salt of the earth' attitude had a huge influence on the young Johnny, who watched her waiting tables, swearing like a trooper and chain smoking.

Johnny Junior, however, had grander ideas. His mother's grandfather was a Cherokee, while relatives on his father's side had emigrated from Germany and Ireland. He always felt that he was different. 'I was a weird kid,' said Depp, who thought that his mixed Cherokee, German and Irish ancestry had marked him out for something special. He particularly enjoyed playing games in which he was the Native American who rebelled against the colonial way of life and, in the process, destroyed everything around him. He liked to keep pet lizards and, on one occasion, was suspended from school for exposing his buttocks to a teacher after she asked him to do something boring. His biggest passion as a child, however, was music; his favourite band were the glamrock masters Kiss. His personal hero was the stuntman, Evel Knievel, who risked life and limb driving over double-decker buses on motorbikes and his bedroom walls were covered with pictures by Vincent Van Gogh, particularly the self-portrait with one ear.

Things changed for Depp when he was just seven years old and the family moved from Kentucky to a working class suburb of Miami in Florida. In his new home, Mira-mar, nothing happened, not even work.

The family lived miserably in a seedy motel for over a year until his father could find a job, an experience that left Johnny Junior permanently scarred and it would be many years before he would ever consider a permanent home.

But Miramar did have some bonuses. Johnny's uncle was a preacher there, in an evangelical gospel group, and Depp loved to turn up at prayer-times and watch his uncle pulling in the crowds with his top performance techniques. Johnny thought it was marvellous the way unbelieving members of the public wandered in, listened and were converted by the power of speech and song. He learnt to imitate many of his uncle's professional oratory skills and soon joined his cousins in their rock gospel group. It was very exciting. His mother bought him an electric guitar for $25 and, at the age of 12, he locked himself inside his bedroom for the best part of a year. When he emerged, he triumphantly declared that he would form a pop band and he would call it 'Flame'. Johnny was now 13. He nipped into his mother's bedroom and stole her crushed velvet shirts which he wore with seersucker bell bottoms. He thought he looked great and he saved desperately for a pair of platform shoes. It was magic.

Depp's third year at high school, consequently, hardly happened. He didn't go to classes, and when he did, he couldn't see the blackboard through his tinted sunglasses. As he admitted himself, he hung around with bad crowds who liked to spend their week-

ends breaking back into school and destroy-
ing the furniture. Occasionally they varied
their schedule by doing a bit of shoplifting
or losing their virginity (Johnny at the age of
13) or doing most of the available drugs in
Florida. 'I wouldn't say I was bad or mali-
cious,' he claimed in an interview, 'I was just
curious . . . but eventually you see where
that's headed and you get out.'

One of the factors that helped Johnny to see
'where that's headed' was the sudden and
acrimonious divorce of his parents just two
years later. It was a profoundly traumatic
time for his mother, for whom this was a
second failed marriage, and Johnny, being
the youngest, was the only child still living
at home and so saw the effects of divorce on
Betty Sue in magnified detail. In a gesture of

solidarity, he not only stayed at home with his mother but had her name tattooed permanently at the top of his left arm, enclosed in a huge red heart; on his right bicep he added a picture of an Indian Chief's head. While Dan and Christi came round to visit often, his other sister, Debbi, went to live with his father, merely adding to the domestic confusion.

Johnny's school performance sank to nothing and he linked up with his friend Sal Jenco, whose parents had also split up. Soon Johnny moved out of the family home and went to live with Sal in the back of his car. It was a 1967 Impala and the two boys hung out, listening to the radio and playing the guitar, stealing sandwiches from the 7-Eleven Shop to get by. Depp stopped

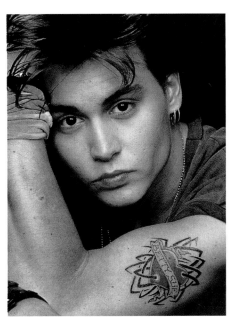

Johnny's 'Betty Sue' tattoo

making even a token effort to go to school and, instead, formed a new band called The Kids. They were dynamite – good-looking, punky, completely wild and crazy – the hottest thing ever to hit the clubs of Miami and soon the local sensation, quickly becoming the support group for all the more important groups who came to town, including Talking Heads and the B52s. Depp was still under age and wasn't officially allowed to play in clubs that served alcohol but the club managers made so much money from the young studs that they would let him in anyway.

By 1983 the band was quite well established and one of the guys in the band introduced Johnny to his sister after a gig. She was a musician, too, and very mature, being a ripe old 25. Lori Ann Allison and Johnny Depp got married within a few months of meeting and soon Lori Ann joined the band. They decided to relocate to Los Angeles where they were bound to find fame and fortune. But success in California wasn't as straightforward as they had hoped. 'There were so many bands it was impossible to make any money,' said Johnny, 'so we all got side jobs. We used to sell ads over the telephone. Telemarketing. We got $100 a week. We had to rip people off.' The band had a few gigs and, once, they even played on the same bill as Billy Idol but generally speaking they weren't going anywhere career-wise and everyone was demoralised. The strain took its toll and, at the tender age of 22, Depp got divorced. His marriage was a failure, his career was yet to flourish and his income was almost non-existent. 1985 wasn't a great year for Johnny Depp.

The good news, however, was that the divorce was amicable and that Lori Ann soon started to date a young actor called Nicolas Cage who just happened to be the nephew of the film director, Francis Ford Coppola. Depp and Cage were soon firm friends and serious drinking buddies and Cage said he thought that Johnny was handsome enough to make it in Hollywood and gave his new chum the name of his own agent. Cage was certainly right about his looks and Depp soon found himself at the audition for his first film, a low-budget horror flick called *A Nightmare on Elm Street*.

MODEST BEGINNINGS

A Nightmare on Elm Street was the dream-child of Wes Craven, who was casting for the role of the heroine's boyfriend. Depp later explained that, 'Wes had written the part of a big, blond, football player guy. And I was sort of emaciated, with old hair-spray and spiky hair and earrings. And then five hours later the agent called me and said, "you're an actor".' Depp's instant success had much to do with the fact that Wes

Craven had used his teenage daughter and her schoolfriends as sex appeal barometers. They had all sat in at the auditions and then had to tell him which boy they fancied the most. Johnny Depp had no competition. 'They absolutely flipped over him,' said Wes and Depp soon found himself on the set playing the part of the heroine's boyfriend who can't stay awake and therefore allows Freddy Krueger, the nightmare man, to kill him in his sleep. It was baptism by fire for the new performer, who had to film his first death scene surrounded by a rotating set with 110 gallons of blood substitute being pumped out of a bed and all over his body. 'I love this stuff,' Depp told *Fangoria* magazine. 'The kid falls asleep and it's all over. His bloody body rises straight out of the bed and then topples over, too. I heard somebody talk about having a dummy shot out of the bed, but I said "Hey, I want to do this! It'll be fun! Lemme do it!".' And so he did it all himself. Apart from his incredible enthusiasm for the gore and his obvious acting ability, Johnny was also the best-looking man on the film set. He was a hugely popular guy.

Shooting finished in July 1984 and Depp made $1,200 a week for his six weeks work. 'Never had I seen anything like that. It was amazing to me that someone wanted to pay me that much money.' The film was even a success critically though it didn't lead to great things straight away. Depp whiled away his under-employed months playing in a band called Rock City Angels, though he forgot to tell The Kids that he was no longer playing with them. 'They were mad,' he said later, 'they probably still hate me.'

Eventually Johnny got work on *Private Resort*, a teen sex comedy which is generally omitted from his CV, and then in a made-for-TV special called *Slow Burn* which also featured the brother of Julia Roberts, Eric. 'I made some awful movies when I was first starting out,' is all that Depp has to say about this period, 'but I'm not embarrassed by them, especially as I didn't think I was going to be an actor – I was just trying to make some money. I was still a musician. I couldn't believe how much they were paying me.' For over a year after *Slow Burn*, Depp didn't get any auditions at all and he was considering abandoning acting

Johnny

altogether when he got offered a part in a new film to be directed by the maverick Oliver Stone. It was to be called *Platoon*.

Stone had written the script ten years earlier, on his return from Vietnam, but it was considered to be anti-American and he couldn't get the necessary financial backing to shoot the movie. After the success of his film, *Salvador*, however, he resuscitated his long-cherished film which would star Charlie Sheen as a 19-year-old soldier who is sent to Vietnam and has a really bad time. 'I went to read for Oliver Stone and Oliver scared the s★★★ out of me!', said Depp but he still got the part. Two and a half months of filming in a jungle in the Philippines might have sounded exciting but the actors were in for a less than glamorous time. The

30 men had to do 13 days of real field training in the bush outside Manila. Depp had to wear fatigues and boots and was issued with a dog tag, a rifle and red night filters. One night he was forced to dig his own foxhole and sleep there. Every day, he had to attend lectures on rifle technology while he sweated in the heat and the constant humidity. Everyone fell ill but the shooting was finally wrapped up on the 54th day as scheduled, though the major disappointment for Depp was that most of his hard work ended up on the cutting-room floor.

Platoon opened in February 1987 and became the highest grossing film of the month, earning over $8.1 million on its first weekend. Later that year, it also picked up a handy four Oscars including Best Picture. As well as his good fortune in having been involved with such a winning film, Depp had also begun dating a very beautiful, would-be actress called Sherilyn Fenn who was later to star in the TV series, *Twin Peaks*. She was just 17-years-old.

Depp was picked for the lead part in a teen series called *21 Jump Street* and he signed on for 13 episodes. Depp had the innate coolness that the series needed to capture the teenage market and played Tom Hanson, an undercover high school cop. Tom is a 25-year-old who looks about 15. He is therefore chosen as the cop who has to infiltrate the local high schools, pretending to be a pupil, and then ferret out the bad kids who deal in drugs. The series, which was shot in

Vancouver, Canada, was a huge success and, though Depp was paid $45,000 per episode, he had to film for 15 hours a day and found it all a bit lonely. After a few months he managed to persuade his mother, Betty Sue, and her new husband to move to Vancouver just to be with him and then he got his childhood pal, Sal Jenco, to come up north too. The production team, in fact, were so impressed with this weird, drop-out friend of the lead actor that they gave him a part in the show, playing a weird drop-out called Blowfish. Eventually Depp even persuaded his girlfriend, Sherilyn Fenn, to join him in Vancouver and arranged for her to have a guest spot in episode nine.

21 Jump Street soon became the show with the highest audience ratings among 18 to 34-year-old American females. Johnny Depp began receiving more fan mail than Charlie Sheen and the production company soon asked him to take part in the teen-mag interview circuit. 'We want you to do these interviews and stuff for magazines,' was how he described this phase in his career, 'and I said, "what magazines?" And they said, "Sixteen! Teen beat! Teen Dream! Teen Poop! Teen Piss! Teen S★★★!".' Depp wasn't impressed but his fan mail kept on growing. The entire cast of *21 Jump Street* was mobbed on a promotional tour of Chicago and the actors were greeted by hordes of screaming teenagers. The only one they really wanted to see was Johnny Depp but the recalcitrant star was whisked away by bodyguards in a large limousine. Despite this lack of enthusiasm he was still voted as one of *Rolling Stone* magazine's 'Hot faces of 1988' and, according to *US* magazine, he was also one of the nation's '10 sexiest bachelors'. Depp couldn't bear it. He couldn't even bear to watch the show, he thought it was such rubbish. He stopped reading the scripts and merely learnt his own words and then turned up for filming. But he had signed up for six series of the show with all the media packaging that went with it and there was little that he could now do, save try to get the sack. He began refusing to do certain episodes on either ethical or critical grounds and he insisted on making the scripts more politically correct. He was 'difficult' on set and did his absolute best to be fired.

But the producers knew a good thing when

they saw it and they wouldn't fire him. Depp was their best asset and they weren't going to let him go without a fight. But they did make a few minor concessions and they allowed him to go behind the camera, for once, and to direct a few public service announcements on such issues as racism and AIDS. He enjoyed the experience and it encouraged him to go on and script his first short film which was called *Every Cake, Neil* and was about 'the things people do that can screw each other up'. The producers didn't really care how he spent his spare time. He was now a teen pin-up idol and a constant focus in girls' magazines – though the labelling fuelled his determination never to return to such trivia once he had managed to make his escape from *21 Jump Street*.

Depp's frustration with his career took its toll on his personal life. Wild, uproarious behaviour was not unknown. One evening, in 1989, he tried to enter a hotel where some of his friends were staying, and after a fight with a security guard, he was arrested and spent the night in Vancouver's central police station. He began appearing in public with numerous starlets, even though he was reported to be engaged to Sherilyn Fenn. His behaviour led to a bumper sticker, popular at the time, which read 'Honk if you haven't been engaged to Johnny Depp'. He was often seen out on the town with Jennifer Grey, who had played the female lead in *Dirty Dancing* but, beyond having a good time, he didn't seem to know where he was going, either personally or professionally.

Johnny in *Cry Baby*

CRY BABY

Maverick film-maker John Waters had risen to notoriety in 1972 when he made a film called *Pink Flamingos* starring an overweight transvestite called Divine. It was labelled in the press as 'surely one of the most vile films ever made' and, as such, Waters was the ideal director for a rebel like Johnny Depp. Johnny learnt that Waters was making a juvenile delinquent love story called *Cry Baby* and he jumped at the chance to be in this fifties spoof. 'More than anything,' said Waters at the time, 'I need actors who can take a step back and laugh at themselves good-naturedly.' He needed a teen idol to play the lead role and, as research, he went out and bought every single teen magazine he could find. Each one featured Johnny Depp on the cover. 'I think he was brave to take this part because he told me that it was the most peculiar script he had ever seen and by portraying Cry Baby [the lead character] he's right out there, making fun of himself,' said Waters. Depp and Waters were made for each other.

With a huge teen star on the payroll, Waters, too, was suddenly playing in a different ball-park. 'They gave me $8 million to make a movie, not $10,000,' he said,

With Amy Locane, *Cry Baby*

frankly stunned. Other diverse actors involved in the production included Ricki Lake, who was a Waters regular at this period; Willem Dafoe, a serious actor who had been in *Platoon*; an ex-porn star called Traci Lords and former terrorist-hostage, Patty Hearst. All these and Iggy Pop, too. Depp loved it and felt liberated at long last. For the first time in his life, he was actively encouraged to contribute to the script and shooting was a very happy time for everyone involved. Waters fulfilled a childhood ambition in having the film selected as an official entry at the Cannes Film Festival. The midnight screening was completely sold out and it received a standing ovation. Depp and Waters became life-long friends and *Cry Baby* was shown all over the world. Though it didn't make much money in the

States, the film did well in Australia and Europe where Depp became a minor celebrity straightaway. More importantly, the film wiped out the dippy teen idol image he'd been trying to get rid of for years. Though he still had one series of *21 Jump Street* left to film, the cinema world was now his oyster.

Winona Horowitz was born on 29 October 1971 in Winona, Minnesota, after which her parents moved to California and joined the hippie trail. Her godfather was the LSD guru Timothy Leary and she began acting at the age of 12. She soon changed her name to Winona Ryder, after her favourite rock star, Mitch Ryder, was quickly spotted by an LA casting agent and soon appeared in films like *Beetlejuice* and *Heathers*. Johnny

Depp met the rising star at the premiere of her new film *Great Balls of Fire* in which she played the teenage bride of Jerry Lee Lewis and, as the couple's eyes met across the cinema foyer, they both knew it was love. 'When I met Winona,' said Depp, 'we fell in love. It was absolutely like nothing ever before – ever. We just started hanging out and we've been hanging out ever since.' Johnny was Winona's first proper boyfriend and the pair had a lot in common including mutual obsessions with J D Salinger's novel *Catcher in the Rye* and the entire works of the beat generation writer, Jack Kerouac.

Their romance was seized upon by the tabloid magazines and, to add fuel to the fire, Johnny was 26 while Winona was still only 17. Once again Depp declared his intention

Winona Ryder

to get engaged. 'Winona is a big help,' he told the press, 'she knows exactly what I'm going through, because she's going through the same thing. I think because we are in love we do feel happy with each other's success.' Depp had a new tattoo burnt into his arm which read, proudly, 'Winona Forever'. Winona herself commented, 'I sort of was in shock. I mean, it's a big thing, because it's so permanent.' She was soon due to star in Francis Ford Coppola's film, *The Godfather Part III* and she had to fly to Rome to begin shooting.

Ryder never even made it past the hotel foyer in Rome. Depp soon showed up in Italy and Winona didn't appear from her room for days, as she had a fever and had been told to rest. She soon returned to the

Paper cut-out demonstration, *Edward Scissorhands*

States to recuperate, but the press were profoundly suspicious. Depp was soon due to start filming *Edward Scissorhands*, his first major mainstream role, and he really wanted his girlfriend to play the part of . . . his girlfriend in the film, Kim Boggs. To do both *The Godfather* and *Scissorhands* would have been impossible and the press drew their own conclusions. 'I don't know why nobody believed the truth,' said Ryder. But they didn't and, miraculously, she recovered from her illness in time to take the role of Kim Boggs. 'Maybe people thought that Johnny was influencing me,' said Ryder, 'but he wasn't.' In any event, the pair were evidently both very enthusiastic about appearing together in a film to be directed by Tim Burton.

Tim Burton was an animator who had won the Disney Fellowship in 1976. He had worked for Disney on various projects since then and made his own animated short called *Vincent*, which told the story of a young boy who wants to be Vincent Price, the horror star. Though the plot and the images were far too disturbing for Disney, the five-minute film went on to win a whole range of awards and to set Burton up for his first feature film, *Pee-wee's Big Adventure*. This was followed by *Beetlejuice* which was a huge success and enabled Burton to direct *Batman*. Burton's main desire, after these big commercial projects, was to return to a small-scale pet project called *Edward Scissorhands*. It was a variation on the Frankenstein theme and would, once again, feature Burton's personal hero, Vincent Price, as the

inventor who dies before he has created
proper hands for his created son. The son,
Edward, is found and adopted by the local
Avon lady and he soon becomes an object of
fascination to the neighbours.

'The character was closest to me,' said
Depp, 'I personally felt that he was a little
boy in the brain. A really small child.' The
studio wanted Tom Cruise to play the role
but Depp had other ideas. 'I realised that it
was something that was only going to come
around once, that I would never see it
again. I felt so attached to this story. Then
reality set in. I was TV boy. No director in
his right mind would hire me to play this
character. I had done nothing workwise to
show that I could handle this kind of role.'
Depp quickly arranged a meeting with

Burton and sat down to watch all of his previous films. The pair met in the lobby of the Bel Age Hotel in LA and neither seemed able to finish a sentence but, still, somehow, they managed to communicate and then they both stood up, shook hands and left. Depp was in awe of Burton who had never heard of him. 'My chances were slim at best,' wrote Depp. 'Better known people than me were not only being considered for the role but were battling, kicking, screaming, begging for it.' He needn't have fretted. After a few weeks Burton rang and said simply, 'You are Edward Scissorhands.'

'He's a very funny, warm guy,' Burton said of his new star, 'he's a normal guy – at least my interpretation of normal – but he's per-

Two kinds of hands, *Edward Scissorhands*

ceived of as dark and difficult and is judged
by his looks, but he's almost completely the
opposite of this perception. So the theme of
Edward . . . was a theme he could relate to.'
After this initial decision, casting the rest of
the roles was easy. The fact that Depp and
Ryder were engaged meant that she was the
natural choice for the love interest and
although he was aware of the dangers of
having a 'love-couple' on the set, Burton
thought that 'they were very professional
and didn't bring any weird stuff to the set.'

The production team took over an entire
housing estate north of Tampa in Florida
and 44 of the 50 houses on the four-year-
old estate were given make-overs for the
movie, including smaller window-frames
and new coats of pastel-coloured paint. It

was the summer of 1990 and the crew was the most exciting thing in Land O'Lakes. Every night the entire town would turn up with picnics and deckchairs and watch the glamorous goings-on. Some even volunteered to be extras in the film. The real success of the film, however, would lie not in the set design but in the acting of the lead character; Depp knew that this responsibility rested on his shoulders. His first step was to throw out half the script because 'Edward is not a human and not a robot and he would cut through everything and have the most honest, pure answer in the world,' or so Depp thought. He turned to the silent films of Charlie Chaplin as research material and drew a lot from the movements of Chaplin's Little Tramp character.

Depp's other major problem was working with the long, metal prosthetic hands. Burton wanted Edward to be both beautiful and dangerous so the finger-blades were made of sharp plastic which shone like stainless steel. Each finger could be moved independently and it took hours of practice not to get the blades caught up in a dangerous tangle. On one occasion, Depp accidentally punctured the skin of one of the other actors and drew blood. It was a stressful time for him, having to concentrate both on these technical difficulties and on his most challenging part yet. But the hard work paid off and the film was hailed by critics as a modern fairy-tale. It took over $54 million in the States alone and Depp's performance, in particular, was rated highly. He picked up a whole new type of fan – the cult cinema audience – and he was now considered a 'real' actor.

Having completed a short cameo in *Freddy's Dead: The Final Nightmare*, as a favour for the team who had first launched his career, Depp's next move was to concentrate on his romance with Ryder. She had been off doing her own thing and the couple were spending more and more time apart . Ryder said, 'I remember us desperately hating being hounded. Every day we heard that we were either cheating on each other or we were broken up. It was like this constant mosquito buzzing around us. These labels were being slapped on me, and I didn't have any life outside of it.' She was linked with both Gary Oldman when filming *Dracula* and with Daniel Day-Lewis on *The Age of*

Innocence; finally, by the spring of 1993 it became obvious that she was going out with the lead singer of Soul Asylum, a man called David Pirner. Depp was devastated. 'It was a really lonely time for me,' he declared, 'I poisoned myself constantly, drinking, no sleep, lots of cigarettes.'

Although Ryder never commented on the reasons for the break-up, merely saying that she had been very young at the time, others claimed that it all fell apart because of Depp's reluctance to commit to marriage. Depp could only blame the press – and launched himself into a permanent hatred of journalists. He claimed that the relationship could have worked if only the two of them had been left alone and allowed to work out their differences in private. In the meantime, he was left with a tattoo which still read 'Winona Forever' and which he spent years trying to get surgically removed, letter by letter. For a while he was branded with the immortal slogan, 'Wino Forever', but his biggest problem was being alone. 'It isn't that much fun,' he said.

MOVING ON

Emir Kusturica was an important Serbian film director who had won the Cannes Film Festival's 'Palme D'Or' for his film *When Father Was Away on Business*. He arrived in the States in 1991 and wanted to make a small film about the American Dream. Depp was thrilled to get the chance to play in another offbeat film with a slightly experimental director; shooting would take place in Alaska, Arizona and New York with such acting luminaries as Jerry Lewis and Faye Dunaway. The pressure was all too much for the sensitive Kusturica who soon suffered a nervous breakdown and had to return to New York but the cast refused to work with any other director.

Depp found a soulmate in his new director and constantly craved the director's attention. The two of them stayed up all night playing loud music, drinking and reading Dostoyevsky, and Faye Dunaway, for one, didn't feel that she was getting the star treatment she expected. Depp insisted on accompanying Kusturica to the Cannes Film Festival in 1992 to promote the unfinished *Arizona Dream,* where he refused to do interviews because he had read somewhere that Brando refused to do interviews.

Depp in *Arizona Dream*

Arizona Dream eventually went on to win the Special Jury Prize at the Berlin Film Festival in 1993 but was only awarded a limited cinema release.

Next came *Benny and Joon* which gave Depp the opportunity to star in an eccentric role and be directed by an unknown who wouldn't cramp his style. Johnny played a young man who falls in love with an emotionally disturbed girl, in a script which the Canadian director, Jeremiah Chechik, described as 'a romance between two oddities who meet and fall in love'. Depp was the obvious choice for the lead character, Sam, who is a big fan of Charlie Chaplin and Buster Keaton and spends his time dressing up like the comics and imitating their routines in the park. Depp was delighted. 'The strange

The 'two oddities' in *Benny and Joon*

thing about *Benny and Joon*,' he said, 'was that here I was doing my salute to Buster Keaton in this MGM movie and MGM was the studio that wrote his career off in the first place.' Depp felt that justice had won through. Joon was played by Mary Stuart Masterson and the film was, in general, positively received, with Depp getting good reviews for his part. But the London *Evening Standard* gave the general concencus on the film as a whole: 'too kooky for words'. It was a success, but a limited one, and Depp's agent began to think that he shouldn't do too many more 'weirdo' pictures.

Johnny, however, had other plans. *What's Eating Gilbert Grape?* was the tale of another lost and naive soul, stuck in small-town America wasting away, until the day a beautiful girl rolls into town and changes everything. Lasse Hallstrom, the Swedish film director who had had a hit with *My Life as a Dog*, saw the film as his chance to produce his vision of America and the writer of the original novel on which the script was based, Peter Hedges, thought that Depp was perfect for the central role. Gilbert Grape's father has committed suicide; his mother is obese and can't get out the house; his brother is mentally handicapped and his two sisters are depressed. The situation only improves when a character called Becky drives into town and is forced to stay because her camper-van has broken. Becky was played by Juliette Lewis (who went on to star in *Natural Born Killers* and *Strange Days*). Depp had a fine old time on the set in Austin, Texas, hanging out with

Johnny and Juliette Lewis in *What's Eating Gilbert Grape?*

The family with problems, *What's Eating Gilbert Grape?*

Hallstrom and learning silly phrases in Swedish. The most awe-inspiring actress in the film, however, was not a professional but a local called Darlene Cates who played the mother, and genuinely hadn't left her house for five years before appearing on a chat show to talk about her obesity problem. 'I hope *What's Eating Gilbert Grape?* helped change people's attitudes and made them more tolerant,' she said later. She certainly made an impact on Depp who said that 'the first time I met Darlene I looked beyond her size and I saw this sweet face and these soulful eyes and I thought she was so beautiful. I found her very brave to unravel her emotional life in front of the whole world – and this from somebody who'd never acted before.' Filming was therapeutic for Depp who said that he 'was trying to escape from my own brain. I didn't know who was who and it was all very confusing.' The film was very confusing for reviewers also, and the consensus was that this was one crazy film too far.

In August 1993 Depp diversified by co-buying a nightclub in LA which rapidly became one of the hottest places in town. The 'Viper Room' could hold only 200 people but many of these were Depp's top Hollywood connections and one of the five booths was reserved permanently for his agent, Tracey Jacobs, who had a gold plaque above her seat which read 'Don't F★★★ With It'. Depp wanted to create a club where he could hear music from Louis Jordan to Velvet Underground and, more importantly, where he could pick up a guitar and have a go if he felt like it. The club was run by his old friend, Sal Jenko. All sorts of people turned up to listen and learn including River Phoenix, already an acting legend and known for his politically correct, hippie life-style.

On 30 October 1993, Phoenix arrived at the 'Viper Room' for a night of fun with his girl-friend, Samantha Mathis, his brother Leaf and his sister Rain. He brought his guitar because he thought he might perform on stage but, just after midnight, River felt ill and was taken outside for fresh air. His brother dialled for an ambulance but, by the time the medics arrived, he was already dead from a drugs overdose.

Depp was immediately on the hostile end of

media attention. 'There was a lot of specu-
lation going on,' said Depp, 'a lot of people
were playing backyard detective and
exploiting the situation . . . I've worked in
this business for ten years and to say I
opened a night club to allow people to do
drugs . . . do people think I'm insane?' He
soon had to deal with a new scandal when
the singer Jason Donovan also collapsed
right outside the club. This one wasn't fatal
but Depp's reputation was sinking. On odd
occasions, now, he could be spotted in the
middle of the night, marching up and down
Sunset Boulevard, handing out fifty and
hundred dollar bills to the homeless, per-
haps this was Depp's way of clearing his
troubled conscience.

By March 1994, Depp's life was looking up

again. At 'Smash Box', a Los Angeles night-club, Depp held a launch for his eight-minute film about the dangers of drugs. It was called *Banter* – a straight-forward anti-drugs promo – and at the party, Depp had a new girlfriend hanging from his arm and she was a supermodel. Kate Moss, the super-thin waif from Croydon in Surrey, was born on 16 January 1974 and 'discovered' at an airport at the age of 14. By 1993 she had a $1 million contract with Calvin Klein, in many of whose adverts she appeared naked. The British press, in particular, had a field day with the new media couple but Depp had washed his hands of journalists. 'As long as they're not hurting my family or someone I love, they can say I have a fetish for midget amputees for all I care,' was his only comment. The pair had met a few weeks earlier at a New York bistro called 'Café Tabac'. Moss had been at a different table with some people he knew and he had called over and asked her to join him. She did and never left. 'She's a real down-to-earth English girl who gives me no chance to get big-headed about my life,' he said.

The age disparity between the two was even greater than it had been between Depp and Ryder but the pair appeared to get along well. They both enjoyed going to funfairs and they both hated journalists. Kate Moss soon became Depp's 'fiancée'. By 1995 her fame almost exceeded his with the publication of a book of photographs of her entitled *Kate*. At the tender age of 21, Moss was earning over £2 million a year. Faye Dunaway said of her friend's new romance: 'He always believes in this pure way about love . . . it's instinctive with him.' One of his former girlfriends, Tally Chanel, said, however, that the first time she met the superstar he asked her to marry him, too.

Kate Moss appeared on British television and said, 'he's really wild but in a nice way. He's always surprising me. He once said to me he had something down his bum but he didn't know what. So I put my hand down his trousers and pulled out a £10,000 diamond necklace.' Depp had to get his kicks somehow since he had now given up alcohol and drugs and he did this by playing in bands with such hard men as the Pogues lead singer, Shane MacGowan, and the ex-Sex Pistols guitarist, Steve Jones. Depp soon signed his new band to Capitol records for

£500,000 and they said that they would produce a record by mid-1996. After all these years, Depp still wanted to be a rock star.

In September 1994, Depp checked into The Mark Hotel in New York since his normal hotel, The Carlyle, was full up. He had come to the city to do the initial publicity work for a new Tim Burton film, *Ed Wood*, for which he had abandoned both Tom Cruise's part in *Interview with the Vampire* and the Keanu Reeves role in *Speed*. Jim Keegan, the night security guard at the hotel, didn't like the look of Depp and he monitored his movements closely. On Monday 12 September 1994, Kate Moss was also in Depp's room and about 5 a.m. in the morning on the 13th, John Keegan heard a series of crashing noises from inside the couple's suite. Within a few seconds, Keegan was outside Room 1410 and told Depp that he would have to leave the hotel or Keegan would call the police immediately. Depp offered to pay for the damage but didn't wish to leave. Keegan called the police. Within half an hour Depp was leaving the hotel in handcuffs, accompanied by three officers from the 19th precinct.

He was released the next afternoon after allegedly being mobbed by female police officers all night. In his witness statement, Keegan listed ten damaged items of furniture but Depp merely said 'it wasn't a great night for me. I'm not trying to excuse what I did or anything like that, because it's someone else's property and you gotta respect that. But you get into a head space

Martin Landau and Johnny, *Ed Wood*

and you're human.' His two charges of criminal mischief left him with a bill of $9,767.12 and he was bound over to keep the peace for 12 months. He was also on the front page of most of the New York newspapers and Depp was convinced that the whole incident was a set-up by the hotel in order to gain themselves some publicity.

But the incident did no harm to Depp's career. Just a month later he made the covers of *People*, *Premiere* and leading gay magazine *The Advocate*. He was also nominated for a Golden Globe award for his part in *Ed Wood*. 'The hotel thing hasn't hurt his career,' John Waters told *Esquire*, 'he looked good under arrest. I loved the handcuffs – they always work. Criminal movie star is a really good look for Johnny.'

ED WOOD

'Can your hearts stand the shocking true story of Edward D Wood Jnr?' began Tim Burton's film biography of the legendary Hollywood director. Ed Wood was a legend outside his own lifetime. He created such dire epics as *Plan Nine from Outer Space* and the first ever transvestite film, *Glen or Glenda* and had often been voted the world's worst film director. He was true cult material.

Tim Burton immediately saw connections between Wood's position in Hollywood and his own. 'There's something beautiful about somebody who does what they love to do, no matter how misguided, and remains optimistic and upbeat against the odds,' he said. He also knew that he had to have Depp to play the lead role. 'I was at home,' said Depp later, 'when Tim called and asked to meet with me right away. He was real secretive: "How quickly can you get to the Formosa cafe?" I go "20 minutes", and I went there. He was sitting at the bar. We sat and had a beer. When he told me about the project, I thought it was an incredible idea. I immediately said "Yes, let's do it". I was at the bar by 8.20. By 8.25 I was committed, completely committed. I was already familiar with Wood's films. I knew that nobody could tell his story better than Tim. Tim's passion became my passion.' Johnny was able to watch Wood's own performance in *Glen or Glenda* and study old footage of Wood in action as a director. He pored over every piece of evidence and the result was the most sophisticated performance of his career. He didn't try to recreate Ed Wood, the man, since he felt that would be a waste of time, he simply attempted to pay homage to someone who really believed in what he did. And he wasn't remotely worried about wearing drag on screen.

Martin Landau won that year's Best Actor Oscar (1995) for his part as Bela Lugosi, and Depp was ecstatic when the real Kathy Wood, Ed's widow, turned up on set unannounced and gave him her dead husband's wallet and phone book. 'It's the first time that I'm actually looking forward to seeing something that I was in,' he said. The film finished shooting in November 1993 but didn't open until October 1994. Though the reviews were very good, it didn't take much money at the box office in the States but, when it opened in the UK in May 1995, it did surprisingly well and got very good reviews for Depp's performance. Depp's career was back on course.

The idea for Depp's next film, *Don Juan de Marco* came from a psychiatrist turned novelist called Jeremy Leven. Leven had no idea who should play the role of the modern Don Juan. When he heard that Johnny Depp was keen to take the part, the director was initially delighted but then learnt that Depp would only do it if Marlon Brando would play the psychiatrist. Leven was incredulous but Depp, now in his thirties, found that he was often described as 'the best actor of his generation' and he, therefore, identified with Brando who had just turned 70.

Don Juan de Marco was being co-produced by Francis Ford Coppola and Leven's incredulity was misplaced. Coppola had directed Brando in *The Godfather* films and Coppola persuaded Brando to take on the role, despite his numerous family problems. He was absolutely charming. He constantly bought drinks for everyone on the set and Depp was in seventh heaven. Faye Dunaway, who played Brando's wife, also enjoyed herself. 'It was tremendously exciting working with Marlon and Faye,' said Depp, 'they are actors with incredible careers. I was privileged to work alongside them and learn. As soon as I saw him he just instantly put me at ease. He became the great, wonderful guy I was working with.' The pleasure of filming showed through in the finished product, with most praise being piled on Depp himself. He was now in an extremely strong position career-wise, but he would have to break through to mainstream films or he would start to lose ground.

In May 1995, he flew to the Cannes Film Festival with Kate Moss at his side. He had another film in the competition besides *Ed Wood* – the poorly received Jim Jarmusch

Western *Dead Man*. In it, Depp plays a weedy accountant called William Blake who finds himself in a Western town called Machine. Filming in the desert had been tricky and the actors could barely see the camera through the dust storms. Jarmusch, who had written the central part especially for Depp, was amazed by his professionalism, saying, 'He really is one of the most precise and focused people I've ever worked with.' Depp was pleased to be able to work with the Hollywood star, Robert Mitchum. Still, the finished film was generally considered to be a bit of a bore and Depp didn't win anything at Cannes. But he enjoyed the experience and *Ed Wood* did very well.

On 9 June 1995, Depp celebrated his 32nd

Brando, Dunaway and Depp, *Don Juan de Marco*

birthday. He was now in the process of filming his first ever real action movie, *Nick of Time*, a big budget remake of *The Man Who Knew Too Much*, a Hitchcock thriller. Depp is a young professional, forced to carry out a political assassination in order to save his child's life. For once Depp was working with a really mainstream director, John Badham, whose previous credits had included *Saturday Night Fever*. Depp said that the concept of the preciousness of parenthood was what drew him to the script, as well as the chance to work with Christopher Walken. Another interesting feature was the documentary feel of the camera work, most of which took place in Union Station in Los Angeles. Most mornings Depp turned up at the station looking like death, but Badham said that he didn't care. 'Why ask the obvious? What I learned right away was that it didn't matter if he never went to bed, he was right on top of it.' Everyone seemed pleased and the film was released in the States in December 1995.

Meanwhile Depp had apparently, and unexpectedly, been offered the chance to star once again with his hero, Marlon Brando. In *Divine Rapture*, Depp was to play a journalist investigating religious miracles in Ireland alongside Debra Winger and John Hurt. Depp set off for the Emerald Isle in the summer of 1995, highly excited at the prospect of this black comedy. Almost immediately it began to pour with rain; filming was stopped and then the Catholic Church forbade the crew from filming in either of the local churches, claiming that Brando's version of an Irish priest made the entire faith look ridiculous.

The 450 residents of the town of Ballycotton in County Cork had been very excited at the prospect of Brando spending some of his $4 million fee in the local shops and Depp told the local press that he thought the town was marvellous, that he had found his roots at last and that he was seriously contemplating becoming an Irish citizen. But the rain continued and nothing happened and Depp pined for the pitbull terrier that Kate Moss had given him which he had named Moo. On 17 July 1995, filming was shut down permanently because nobody had secured the $16 million needed to make the film; $1 million had already been given to Brando which had crippled the rest of the minimalist bank account. On 24 July, the film was officially cancelled and all cheques were declared void. 'In spite of the continuing assurance of financial backing from our backer,' read the official statement, 'the funds have not been forthcoming.' The cast and crew weren't the only people now out of pocket. The Bay View Hotel was owed money for 20 bedrooms and the local fishermen were all feeling short-changed. The film was a fiasco; the flashy Hollywood crowd were seen as a bunch of no-hopers and everybody was fed up. Brando, at least, promised that he would personally meet the costs of his gardener, cook and two housekeepers for the rest of his stay – which was precisely two days. Depp had already left. He went away for a weekend with Kate on 17 July and never bothered to come back. He didn't get paid for his few pitiful scenes and years of legal wrangling will, no doubt, ensue.

Depp returned to his many other unformed plans. He might do a British film called *The Cull*. He was quite keen on a Francis Ford Coppola project to make a film of Jack Kerouac's *On the Road* – so keen, in fact, that he spent $9,300 at a celebrity auction on a raincoat that Kerouac had worn once. He also thought he might make a film called *Donnie Brasco* with Al Pacino but this is still a very vague prospect.

In the meantime Depp wanted to start directing. He had already made a pop video

Johnny Depp

for his old friend, Shane MacGowan of The Pogues, and he had co-directed an 11-minute short called *Stuff*, and now had plans to work on his first feature with his brother, Dan. It would be based on a novel by Gregory MacDonald called *The Brave* – the tale of a Native American who sacrifices his own life in order to save his family. Other plans included buying his first ever permanent home, after his own rented house was damaged in the Los Angeles earthquake. In October 1995 he purchased, for $2.3 million, Bela Lugosi's former mansion, a 9,000 sq. ft. estate called 'The Castle'.

Depp now had a home, even if it was a bizarre Gothic one with a warped history, and he claimed he was keen to start a family.

He didn't, however, seem to want to stop travelling or filming and Kate Moss wasn't anywhere near Los Angeles. The British newspapers announced that the pair had split up and, with Kate on the catwalks in New York, Depp retreated to his mansion where he was spotted with a variety of anonymous nymphets. Depp claimed that it was Kate's problem and that she was 'immature', (she was still only 21), though he wasn't exactly behaving like a regular, family guy. He had been a teen idol, a pop star and an accomplished actor. He wasn't sure of his future direction and stayed in Los Angeles to contemplate what lay ahead. 'The tragedy,' said his *Arizona Dream* co-star, Vincent Gallo, 'is that if he would only allow himself to be who he really is, then he would be a great person, a great talent. He is one of the most funny, talented, likeable, sweet, authentic people I've ever met.'

FILMOGRAPHY

The year refers to the first release date
of the film

1984 A Nightmare on Elm Street
1985 Private Resort
1986 Slow Burn
1986 Platoon
1987 21 Jump Street (TV series)
1990 Cry Baby
1990 Edward Scissorhands
1991 Freddy's Dead: The Final Nightmare
1991 Arizona Dream
1993 Benny and Joon

1993 What's Eating Gilbert Grape?
1994 Ed Wood
1994 Don Juan de Marco
1995 Dead Man
1995 Nick of Time

As Sam in Benny and Joon

ACKNOWLEDGEMENTS

Aquarius
Constellation/Hachette et Cie (courtesy Kobal)
Jersey Films (courtesy Kobal)
Kobal Collection
MGM (courtesy Kobal)
New Line/Zoetrope (courtesy Kobal)
Paramount (courtesy Kobal)
Touchstone Pictures (courtesy Kobal)
20th Century Fox (courtesy Kobal)
Universal (courtesy Kobal)